THE MOST IMPORTANT MINISTRY

THREE

MARYS

PETER JOHN BROOKS

THREE MARYS: The Most Important Ministry

ISBN: 978-1-968804-03-9

Published by Fivestone New Media

www.bethelcornerstone.org

Contents

Who can find a virtuous woman? For her price is far above rubies.

Introduction

THREE MARYS impacted the world in a profound way: the mother of Jesus, Mary Magdalene, and Mary of Bethany.

Mary, the mother of Jesus, brought forth the seed of the woman that crushed the head of Satan (Genesis 3:15). As a result of her faithful submission to God, Mary obtained a testimony that reverberates around the world. She said, "All generations will call me blessed" (Luke 1:48b). This prophecy has been fulfilled, as Christians all over the world recognize the blessedness of Mary, mother of Jesus.

The second Mary, Mary Magdalene, overcame great hardship to become one of Jesus' brightest followers. She was the first disciple to see Jesus after his resurrection, and the fact that God granted this privilege to her reveals her importance to God.

The third Mary, from Bethany, anointed Jesus with expensive perfume at just the right moment. This prophetic act, done a few days before his crucifixion, had such an impact on Jesus that he said, "Wherever this gospel is preached in the whole world, what this woman has done will also be told as a memorial to her" (Matthew 26:13b).

The stories of these three women are important accompaniments to the gospel, and they shed light on what happened when God became a man.

"The Word became flesh and dwelt among us" (John 1:14).

The Incarnation is a source of supreme spiritual power. God became a man and died on the cross, unleashing righteousness and salvation into the earth. The creation had been gashed by evil, and no one could heal this wound except God. Jesus died and rose again, shattering sin, death, and Satan. He reconnected heaven to earth, weaving God back into the human story.

The Incarnation revealed God's humility. Christ became a man. He was hungry, thirsty, and tired. He needed a place to eat and a bed to sleep on. As God, Jesus could have met all his needs through divine power, turning stones into bread or pulling water from thin air. But Jesus often didn't work miracles to fill up his lack. He left his own needs unmet, leaving room for people to serve him instead.

The three Marys stepped in. They helped Jesus, encouraged him, cared for him, and understood him. They were extraordinary disciples, not because they preached to crowds or worked miracles, but because they ministered to God.

The stories of these women teach us the important lesson that true discipleship is not about serving ourselves. It's not even primarily about serving others. True discipleship is about serving Jesus.

A Note to the Reader:

Dear friend, it is impossible to know with certainty how some of the events happened in the lives of these three women. But when we combine the perfect testimony of the Bible with cultural clues, it is possible to deduce important truths. With the Bible as our guide, let us go on a journey together, back to the lives of these women, and consider how some astounding Biblical events probably happened.

Part 1.

Mary, Mother of Jesus

You will show me the path of life: in your presence is fullness of joy; at your right hand are pleasures for evermore.

Psalm 16:11

MARY WAS A YOUNG WOMAN who loved God more than anything. To her, the invisible things of heaven were more attractive than the things of the earth. She knew God was the best, most magnificent, most glorious person in the world. No one could satisfy the longings of her heart except God.

Mary prayed. To her, prayer was not a religious duty, but it was something exciting, something *alive*. Prayer put her in touch with God. It opened her eyes to heaven. It made her aware of spiritual things - things that were more real to her than the things of the earth.

Mary prayed for many things, but like many Jews, she probably prayed especially for the Messiah. In Mary's day, Jewish anticipation for the Messiah had reached a fever pitch. The Jews thought their Messiah (*Christ* in Greek) would come at any moment, overthrow Rome, and make Israel the head of the nations.

Mary, like most Jews, didn't know exactly how the Messiah would come, but she probably expected him to arrive from heaven in a blaze of glory. Angels would light up the sky! Glory would flood the world! His arrival would astound everyone, and there would be miracles everywhere. What a wonderful day that would be!

A Life Interruption

One day Mary saw an angel. She had heard about angels from the Bible, but actually seeing an angel was very different from hearing about them. Angels are powerful, bright, and strong. Mary must have been almost overwhelmed by the sight.

The angel said, "Rejoice, highly favored one, the Lord is with you; blessed are you among women!" (Luke 1:28b).

Mary had found favor with God. That's why the angel came to her. Favor is the precursor to revelation. God shows himself to those he favors.

Mary found favor because she was humble. God once told Isaiah, "I dwell in the high and holy place, with him who has a contrite and humble spirit" (Isaiah 57:15b).

God spends time with the humble. He reveals himself to them and speaks to them, because they delight to see him and love to hear his voice.

Mary had a meek and quiet spirit, and that made her submissive to God. "A meek and quiet spirit is in the sight of God of great price" (1 Peter 3:4 KJV).

The meek humbly submit to God, and the quiet hear his voice. These are the ones God speaks to, the ones who hear his word. Through them he accomplishes his will in the earth.

There were many Jewish girls in Mary's day, and there had been millions of young women before her. But Mary was the one who, more than any other, was willing to be molded, shaped, and filled with God. She was the one God had been waiting for.

The angel was named Gabriel, and he said,

> Do not be afraid, Mary, for you have found favor with God. And behold, you will conceive in your womb and bring forth a Son, and shall call His name Jesus. He will be great, and will be called the Son of the Highest; and the Lord God will give Him the throne of His father David. And He will reign over the house of Jacob for-

ever, and of His kingdom there will be no end. (Luke 1:30-33)

Surprised by Revelation

Mary's prayers for the Messiah were being answered, but in a totally different way than she had probably imagined. The Messiah was going to come to the world - via her womb! Mary was becoming the means by which her own prayers would be answered.

> God sometimes turns us into the answer to our own prayers.

She must have been stunned. How could the Messiah be a baby? He was supposed to be a glorious king who would conquer Rome. How could a baby save the world?

Besides that, how could she get pregnant? She wasn't even married! "Mary said to the angel, 'How can this be, since I do not know a man?'" (Luke 1:30).

The angel explained that Mary would become pregnant not by a man, but by the Holy Spirit. The fulfillment of God's word didn't need the intervention of man, it just needed the power of God.

> And the angel answered and said to her, 'The Holy Spirit will come upon you, and the power of the Highest will overshadow you; therefore, also, that Holy One who is to be born will be called the Son of God.' (Luke 1:35)

16

A Holy Invasion

The Holy Spirit shall come upon you.

The Holy Spirit accomplishes God's will in the earth. When the Spirit of God shows up, God's will is done. God's power will bring God's word to pass. In the original Greek, the word that is translated *come* is much more powerful than in English. It could be translated as *attack*. Mary was about to be invaded by God.

The power of the Highest shall overshadow you.

The word *power* in Greek is *dunamis*. This is the word from which we get *dynamite*. The power of God is like spiritual dynamite that disrupts the normal ways of this world by revealing the power of God.

The word translated as *overshadow* means *to envelope in a haze of brilliance*. This is the same word that was used to describe the transfiguration of Jesus. "He was transfigured before them. His face shone like the sun, and His clothes became as white as the light" (Matthew 17:2).

Something powerful was about to happen to Mary. She was going to be transformed by the power of God.

> God's power always accompanies God's word.

God's word comes to pass in the earth by God's power. We need to submit to him, and as we do, his power is revealed, which will bring his word to pass. God's power always accompanies God's word. This is why his word is alive - it has life within itself. We don't need to rely on ourselves to make God's word effective. We don't need to come up with clever plans to bring it to pass. God will do what he said, if we can just believe.

This union between God and Mary was unprecedented. Whereas God worked through prophets like Moses to accomplish awesome things, this was different. The embryo of Christ was going to be planted inside Mary's virgin womb. Through her, the Seed of the woman was going to come into the world and crush the head of Satan.

Questions

As the angel Gabriel stood before her, thoughts must have tumbled through Mary's mind.

"Will it hurt? What will this mean for my future? What will my parents say? What will my fiancé say?"

Gabriel's message was not a dictatorial command to an overpowered young girl. God was not going to force Mary to get pregnant with his child. But God knew that Mary wouldn't refuse him. God knows all things— past, present, and future. He knew how Mary would respond before he asked her. He knew that Mary, above all other women, was willing to submit to his word. The Holy Spirit had been working in Mary's heart, preparing her for this very moment.

God knew that Mary would choose him, and that's why he chose her.

Mary didn't understand all the implications of obeying God's word, but she didn't need to. Mary knew that God is good, and his word is perfect. Whatever happened as a result of obedience to his word would be God's responsibility, not hers. She didn't need to understand everything, for God would take care of her and watch over his word to perform it.

Mary gave her reply:

"Behold, the handmaiden of the Lord. Let it be done unto me according to your word" (Luke 1:38a).

We don't know exactly when or how it happened, but at some point the power of God flooded into Mary, and the word of God became flesh inside a young woman.

Trouble Strikes

Mary had encountered God, but she wasn't in heaven yet. She was still living on the earth, in a family, among a society. She quickly discovered, as countless girls have discovered throughout history, that it's not easy to be pregnant when you're not married.

Mary's parents must have been shocked when they found out she was pregnant. "How did you get pregnant, girl!?"

Mary denied being with any man. She had just been with God. She wasn't doing anything wrong, she was just praying.

She tried explaining, "I'm not pregnant by a man. I'm still a virgin. When I was praying I got pregnant."

The truth only seemed to make matters worse. Mary's explanations must have sounded insane. Worse, they would have sounded blasphemous.

"I got pregnant by God."

People wanted to kill Jesus for claiming to be the Messiah. Some people might have wanted to kill Mary for asserting that her child was the Messiah.

"Please, believe me! Mom, Dad, don't you trust me?"

The whispering spread. In a close-knit society like Mary's, gossip could be deadly. To be accused of adultery was probably the worst thing that could have happened to her. It wasn't just her reputation that was damaged; it was potentially her life. There were ancient laws about stoning dishonorable girls.

The precious child in Mary's womb was under a cloud. If abortion had been common in those days, the fetal Jesus would have been a prime candidate for early termination. In fact, there were ancient methods of abortion. It is possible that Mary had to fight off angry relatives who wanted her to take an herb or undergo a practice that would expel the "illegitimate" child from her womb. Mary had to protect the word God had given her.

The powerful revelation of God brought the best thing and the worst thing into Mary's life at the same time. One day she was being visited by an angel and being told she's highly favored, the next day her name is being dragged through the mud through charges of immorality. First, God overshadowed her and filled her with himself, then Satan covered over her life with slander!

> The revelation of God can bring both the best thing and the worst thing into one's life, all at the same time.

Mary was probably embroiled in scandal that left her reeling. She didn't know what to do. She must have felt helpless.

Things went from bad to worse. Mary was betrothed to a carpenter named Joseph. Joseph, hearing the news that his fiancé was pregnant, was shocked. He knew that he wasn't the father. How could Mary betray him like this?

Mary probably tried telling Joseph what had happened. She explained how she had been visited by an angel and been moved upon by the Holy Spirit. "It's true, Joseph. The Messiah is in my womb!"

Joseph couldn't believe it. He used to respect Mary's spirituality, but not anymore. He probably thought she had lost control of herself in a moment of weakness and was trying to cover her tracks with outlandish religious excuses.

When Mary's parents first heard about her pregnancy, they might have assumed that she and Joseph had been spending too much time together. But with Joseph denying everything, they were probably as upset as ever.

Joseph knew that marrying an immoral girl might ruin his life. He decided to break off the betrothal.

"Then Joseph her husband, being a just man, and not wanting to make her a public example, was minded to put her away secretly" (Matthew 1:19).

Young Mary was like a tiny boat being capsized in a hurricane. Where was God? Didn't he care? Why didn't he do something?

This was not the blessing that Mary had been promised. This was a cursing. Her reputation was being tattered, and her life was threatened. Her own parents were doubting her, and her relatives probably thought she was evil. To top it off, she was about to be divorced before ever really getting married!

Mary believed God, and suddenly her life was a total wreck!

The Challenge of Obedience

Obedience can be hard. God's word cuts across the world, bringing upheaval to our lives, families, and communities. There are times when the word of God backs us into a corner and leaves us with no way out except that God comes through. We can't think our way out. We need God to open a door, or we'll be overcome.

> For my thoughts are not your thoughts, nor are your ways my ways, saith the LORD. For as the heavens are higher than the earth, so are my ways higher than your ways, and my thoughts than your thoughts. (Isaiah 55:8-9)

That's humbling. It means that we're often not going to understand how God is leading us. We know that God is always good, and that his plans for us are the best. But the fact remains that God's ways and plans are different from our own. If we can't understand how God is leading us, how much less will other people understand?

"Why are you doing that?"
"God told me to do it."
"What do you mean, God told you?"

If you can't really understand it yourself, how can you explain it to someone else? People don't usually question a decision to do something because of money, education, or human relationships. If you move somewhere to get a higher salary, then that's understandable. But doing something because God said to do it? That's incomprehensible for most people.

Through societal pressure, the devil will try to discourage us from following God. He wants to get us to abandon the word of God before it comes to fruition. "Why do you want to ruin your life with that fetal 'thing'? It's not even a baby. It's not a person." He will try to get us to abort the word of God, give up, and return to 'normal' life. "Why do you want to do something *that* crazy? Did God *really* tell you to do that?"

The devil loves it when people give up on God's word before it is manifested into the world. It's like a spiritual abortion, destroying the seed of God's word before it can be manifested to the world.

Sometimes the only way to protect the word of God within us is to withdraw a bit and let the word of God gestate within us for a while.

This is the struggle that Mary was facing. All she could do was pray. She couldn't get any help from people. She needed God to come through.

Deliverance

Even though it seemed like everyone was against Mary, God was on her side. And when a person is facing a spiritual battle, God is the only one she needs to win. At what seemed like the last moment, God spoke to Joseph in a dream. He told him to take Mary as his wife. God told Joseph that the baby in her womb really *was* the Messiah. Finally, Joseph believed what Mary had probably been telling him all along.

When news of their wedding spread, people probably concluded that Joseph and Mary had gotten a little too close before marriage. *That's* why Mary was pregnant (see Luke 3:23). They could understand that. Fornication they could understand, but they couldn't understand God.

Nine Months to Think

Mary had nine months to contemplate the growth of the Messiah in her womb. She probably thought about the things that most pregnant mothers think about, but with a divine twist.

What kind of child would the Messiah be?
Would he cry a lot? Maybe he would never cry, and he would smile and just sit there all placid and calm.
Would he look different from other children?
Would there be a lot of miracles?
What would he be like when he grew up?

Mary pondered the possibilities as the word of God grew within her.

As the baby grew in her womb, Mary also grew. She became bigger and clumsier, stretching in ways she didn't think possible. She couldn't fit into the clothes she used to fit into. The covering that covered her before could cover her no longer. As we believe the word of God, we grow. We may outgrow some spiritual environments and need to find another one that suits us better.

As Mary's pregnancy progressed, her appetite changed. She began eating more food. Her taste probably changed. These changes mirrored her spiritual growth. She probably needed new, fresh bread from heaven. She needed fresh revelation from God.

The growing word of God began to control Mary's schedule, her desires, and her habits. People probably noticed the changes in Mary and remarked that she had become different. She wasn't the same girl she used to be.

> The word of God comes to transform our lives.

The word of God comes to bring complete transformation. When we accept it, it will totally transform our lives.

Challenges of Delivery

At the end of nine months, the Messiah was ready to be born. But at that very moment, when Mary was *very* pregnant and probably felt she couldn't get any bigger, she suddenly had to travel! The government was conducting a census. The young couple had to go to Bethlehem - Joseph's hometown - to be enrolled in a government registry.

Mary and Joseph had no choice, so they packed their bags and began walking to Bethlehem. Maybe they had a donkey, but even so, a donkey wouldn't have made travel much easier. Donkeys are slow, bouncy, and uncomfortable, especially for a woman who is nine months pregnant. The journey from Nazareth to Bethlehem was about 80 miles. It would have taken days. The young couple had to find food and lodging in unfamiliar places.

They probably wondered why God allowed the census to happen at that time. Didn't he have power over these things? Why didn't he cause this census to happen later, after the delivery?

They finally reached Bethlehem. They must have been exhausted. It was probably night. They needed a place to stay, and there was no vacancy at the Bethlehem inn. There didn't seem to be any relatives who would take them in. They didn't know what to do.

The innkeeper, seeing that Mary was pregnant, took pity on the young couple. He allowed them to take shelter in his barn.

They went into the barn and dropped their luggage on the dirt, surrounded by donkeys, sheep, and cows.

This accommodation was uncomfortable, smelly, and it probably tested their faith. Tired from traveling and forced to stay in a barn like animals, they might have doubted God. It was all so hard.

Mary might have wondered, "Why God? Isn't the child in my womb your Son? Why don't you take care of us? We've already been through so much because of your word. Why are we still having so many problems? Why did we have to travel now? Couldn't you at least have arranged a room for us to stay in? Why can't things be more comfortable? Easier? We've already been through so much, Lord..."

They tried to relax in the barn amidst the animals, as best they could.

Suddenly, Mary's body told her in unmistakable terms that she was about to deliver the child. With no one to help them and the animals looking on, in the middle of the barn in a strange town, Mary went into labor.

Out came Christ.

Joseph caught the slippery child, cut his umbilical cord, and laid the Messiah in an animal feeding trough. What inglorious circumstances for the arrival of the King of Kings!

Fruit

The word of God is given so it cannot just be thought about or talked about. We can be spiritually pregnant with the word of God for a long time - but that's not enough.

The word must come out into the world and be implemented in order for it to accomplish the purpose for which God sent it. God wants all visions that he gives to his children to become earthly realities. The word of God must become flesh.

> The invisible word of God must put on flesh in order to accomplish its purpose on earth.

When God's word puts on flesh, the circumstances will usually seem far from ideal. There will be many challenges. When the word is finally revealed, it sometimes looks very small.

Don't despise the day of small beginnings (Zechariah 4:10). That tiny word contains the infinite power of Almighty God. The earth will bend in submission to it.

Confirmation

Mary must have been exhausted. She fumbled around and tried to nurse the Messiah.

Suddenly there was a knock at the barn door. It creaked open and black night poured in, along with a ragtag group of men. Joseph and Mary didn't know what to expect. They were in an unfamiliar area and might have suspected foul play.

But the radiant look on the visitor's faces quickly dispelled the young couple's fear. They listened in awe as these shepherds described seeing angels and hearing a beautiful song about the Messiah. These men had come to worship their Son!

In the midst of gut-wrenching challenges, here was a much-needed sign that God was with them. Glory shone in the midst of night. Angels sang in the midst of hardship. The holy presence of God was revealed in the middle of a dirty barn. Joseph and Mary had gone through so much together with maybe everyone doubting them except cousin Elizabeth… Finally, God gave public confirmation of the private truth they had both heard from God.

Later, wise men from the East came and told Mary and Joseph about a heavenly sign that declared the birth of their holy child. These regal men brought gold, frankincense, and myrrh— valuable gifts, fit for a king. These mysterious visitors with their unusual gifts further encouraged the faith of the young parents.

Ministering to the Word

From before the beginning of the world, the eternal Son of God dwelled in infinite light. He created the universe with a word. He spun galaxies into space and wrote the laws of nuclear reactions.

Now he was a crawling baby. He couldn't walk or talk. He couldn't eat or put on his shirt. Christ had poopy diapers and probably peed on the floor.

[Jesus] made Himself of no reputation, taking the form of a bondservant, and coming in the likeness of men. And being found in appearance as a man, He humbled Himself. (Philippians 2:7-8a)

Jesus emptied himself of his glory so he could become like us.

Mary was now responsible to take care of the Second Person of the Trinity. She nursed him, clothed him, and put him to sleep. And she did more than take care of his physical needs. She taught him. Jesus had a lot to learn. He wasn't born with a grown man's brain. He needed to grow both physically and intellectually.

If Mary had not fulfilled her motherly responsibilities, how would Jesus have survived? How would he have grown? If she hadn't ministered to Jesus, how could he have accomplished God's plans? In ministering to Jesus, Mary helped lay the foundation for his ministry to the world.

Mary and Jesus prayed together. Imagine the exhilaration of Mary, who had once prayed *for* the Messiah, to actually pray *with* the Messiah sitting on her lap? The mother and child must have enjoyed rapturous times together in God's presence.

The word of God originates in heaven with God, and then he gives his word to people. The word of God takes root in the earth when people have faith in it. It shapes the world when people obey it. The word of God grows and prospers in the earth as it is tended by people, just as Jesus grew under the tender care of his mother.

Change

Years went by. Changes to Mary's relationship with her son were coming. The word of God was growing up - beyond Mary's ability to understand it. And when Jesus was 12 years old, Mary saw just how big these changes were going to be.

Mary, Joseph, and many of their relatives had come together to Jerusalem to worship. When they were returning to their hometown, Nazareth, Mary and Joseph thought Jesus was somewhere in the large group of relatives - maybe with the other children. But after traveling for a while, they suddenly realized that he was missing. They couldn't find Jesus anywhere!

They rushed back to Jerusalem. For three days, they frantically looked for him. This wasn't just their boy they had lost. This was the Savior of the world. They must have been in a panic. Maybe they were worried that Satan had somehow killed him.

Finally, after three days, they found Jesus in the temple. He was discussing things with the religious leaders.

Mary asked Jesus why he had left them like this. She told him how upset they all were. How could he do this to them?

> And he said unto them, 'Why did you seek me? Did you not know that I must be about my Father's business?' And they did not understand the statement which he spoke to them. (Luke 2:49-50)

Jesus had been in the temple asking questions of the religious leaders. His heavenly Father must have told him to go to the temple, so he did. Maybe he was learning about their doctrines. By now he was old enough to know the word of God. Maybe he was comparing their religion with what the Bible says, learning details that would inform his ministry when he would later come into the temple as a man.

This was an important event for Jesus. It was essential preparation for him to fulfill his calling. Maybe he had told his parents that God wanted him to go to the temple, but they didn't listen to him. But Jesus had to go to the temple anyway, for his Father told him to. He had to obey God rather than men.

After this event, Jesus returned with his parents to Nazareth. He submitted to them and worked at his father's trade. But Mary and Joseph could no longer fully understand their boy.

The word of God has a life of its own, and it will often be beyond our ability to fully understand it. It will certainly be beyond our control.

Full Manifestation

When Jesus was about 30 years old, he was filled with the Holy Spirit and began working miracles. Mary looked on in awe. Finally, after over 30 years of waiting and believing, her Son was now acting like the Messiah. She had believed it would happen with the eyes of faith, and now she was seeing it come to pass. She must have been thrilled.

Other people quickly began to believe what she knew all along. Jesus began gathering followers, and his ministry gathered momentum.

Mary was exhilarated as the word of God was being fulfilled before her eyes. Her son was healing the sick, casting out demons, raising the dead, and restoring people to God. He was crushing the head of Satan and demolishing the devil's dominion over the earth. Mary rejoiced to see the glorious conquests of her powerful son.

But as exhilarating as all the miracles were, there were challenges too.

One time Mary asked Jesus to assist some people who had come to her for help. Jesus said, "Woman, what have I to do with thee?" (John 2:4 KJV).

This was a slight rebuke. Chastened, Mary hastily turned to the people who asked her for help and said, "Whatever He says to you, do it" (John 2:5b). Mary got the hint and pointed them to her son. If they were to encounter God, it would have to be through Jesus.

Another time, Jesus seemed to not even acknowledge that Mary was his mother. Mary and Jesus' brothers were calling for Jesus to come to them. When someone told him that his mother and brothers stood outside calling for him, he replied, "Whoever shall do the will of God, the same is my brother, and my sister, and mother" (Mark 3:35). Jesus seemed to prefer his own disciples above his mother.

These were hard experiences for Mary, but they helped her understand that unless she believed in Jesus for her own salvation, she would not enter the kingdom of God. As pious as she was, Mary was a sinner who needed a Savior just like everyone else. She needed to understand that Jesus was not just her son; he was God. Mary needed to transition from motherhood to discipleship. Just like everyone else, she had to submit to Jesus, believe the gospel, and be born again. At some point, Mary understood.

Crisis

Jesus had always skirted controversy. He seemed to always be at odds with some influential person or another. He and the world just didn't seem to get along. Mary had seen the confrontations and heard the whispers. She knew that powerful people were plotting to destroy her son.

Up to now, Jesus had always been one step ahead of his enemies. No one had been able to bring him down. But during the third year of his ministry, the threats against him were getting louder and louder. Mary probably kept hoping that Jesus would continue increasing in power, confounding the rulers with the strength of God. She kept praying for him and believing that he would triumph over all opposition.

But suddenly, around Passover, Mary heard news that no mother wants to hear.

Her Son had been arrested.

It happened so fast. There was hardly time for her to think, much less do anything. Not that she could have done anything anyway.

Jesus was rushed to trial. He was pronounced guilty. No one spoke up for him at the judgment seat. No one took his side. He was left alone.

He was brutally beaten by soldiers. Her Son!

Mary may have remembered the prophetic words of old Simeon, whom she had met in the temple when he was a baby, "A sword will pierce your own soul" (Luke 2:35b).

Mary saw her beloved Son walking down the road to the place of execution. Why did he have to die? What had he done wrong? He had helped so many people! How could the leaders of her nation do this to him? To their Messiah? To God!?

Blood dripped from seemingly all parts of his body. Ribbons of flesh hung off him, and huge red welts sprung up and swelled on his back.

She staggered after him to Golgotha, helpless. She watched them drive nails through her Son into wood. As the soldiers heaved the cross up and into the ground, his body was wracked with excruciating pain. She could see the agony all over his face. She knew that face. The face of her boy was twisted under the weight of the sins of the world.

He hung on the cross. After a while, he could hardly breathe. He began to suffocate.

His mother could hardly watch. Her faith was shaken to its core. She knew she had received a word from God. She had believed that word when the whole world seemed against it. She had protected that word and brought it into the world through faith. The word grew up into a boy, and she nourished that boy. She prayed for that precious boy and encouraged him. She told him about how God would never fail, about God's great love. Her boy had become a man and amazed the world with the miracles of God.

Now her strong son was almost dead.

For what seemed like an eternity, she watched him there, hoping that God would come through, hoping that her son would come down and show the world it was all a lie. Maybe she hoped mighty Gabriel would come and set him free.

The beloved disciple John was there. Jesus told John to look after Mary, his mother (John 19:26).

Mary knew what this meant. It was over. Jesus was going to die.

Her son's plaintive cry pierced the air, "My God, My God, why have you forsaken me?" (Matt. 27:46b).

The words ran like a cold steel sword through Mary's heart. Why would the heavenly Father ignore his beloved son?

The life probably seemed to drain from her body. Her prayers seemed to bounce off of a cold and brassy heaven. The world became dark.

Her beloved son died. The angel stopped the knife when Abraham's beloved son Isaac was about to become a sacrifice. Why didn't angels come and stop this cruel death and rescue her son? Wasn't he the real Seed of Abraham?

> The word of God often faces inexplicable opposition in the earth.

She had invested her life for three

decades into this precious word from God. Now that word was dead.

Tested

Overcome, Mary rushed away. It was all too much to bear. She couldn't take any more. She probably ran back to her prayer closet— the place where this journey began about 34 years ago. She began crying out to God.

She was facing a test of faith like she had never faced before. Maybe she faintly remembered the words her son had spoken about his own resurrection. When would it happen? Would it be now, or 1,000 years later?

She must have struggled desperately to hold onto God. Tears, emotional turmoil - she let it all out in prayer. Where was God? Why didn't he answer her? Why was he silent? It was the darkest night she ever faced.

Maybe she recounted testimonies of God's faithfulness. Maybe she thought back to the beginning, to the crisis of her pregnancy. She was in a terrible situation, and everyone was against her, but God came through. In the barn, when she had delivered the child and her body was exhausted, God publicly confirmed her faith with a glorious angelic display.

Time and time again, Jesus had confounded his enemies and proved that he was the Son of God.

> Blind faith holds onto God when everything screams to let go.

He had just raised Lazarus from the dead. She tried remembering the good things. She clung in desperation to a God who had not failed…yet.

The hours dragged on. Night turned into morning. Mary kept desperately praying.

Night fell again. Mary was probably near the point of mental, physical, and emotional exhaustion. She just couldn't find God anywhere in this darkness. She kept reaching out to him and calling out to him. Everything was black. There was no answer but silence.

The morning of the third day, Mary probably had no strength left. Maybe she was on the verge of totally breaking down.

Suddenly, she heard the news.

Jesus was alive.

He had come back from hell. He had crushed Satan. He had defeated death. He was walking around!

Mary probably rushed out and ran around trying to find him. She wanted to see him for herself.

Soon she found him. Her Son. Her God.

Mary understood what it all meant. Her son had to die to pay for the sins of the world.

A Blessed Woman

Mary had prophesied that "all generations will call me blessed" (Luke 1:48b). This prophecy has been fulfilled. Mary obtained a testimony that has rung throughout history. Her faith in God's word unleashed an unparalleled revelation of God to the world. Through faith she saw the invisible word of God until it became a visible Word that took on flesh and delivered the world from sin and evil.

Through faith, Mary opened a door on the earth for God to do what he wanted to do. This is what genuine faith does. It opens the door for God to act.

Sometimes admiration for Mary is taken to an extreme, and people worship her. This is wrong. Mary was a human, like you and me. It is wrong to worship her or pray to her. Only God is worthy of worship. Only God can answer prayer. Neither Mary, nor any other dead saint, can help us now. Mary cannot and will not communicate with us. Any spirit that pretends to be Mary that communicates with anyone is a demon.

One time a woman came to Jesus and tried to praise Mary. "And it happened, as he spoke these things, that a certain woman from the crowd raised her voice and said to him, 'Blessed is the womb that bore you, and the breasts which nursed you!'" (Luke 11:27).

It's as though this woman was trying to worship Mary, his mother.

Jesus didn't encourage this woman's misplaced devotion. He directed her to God. Jesus answered, "More than that, blessed are those who hear the word of God and keep it" (Luke 11:28).

Jesus said that if someone obeys God, he or she can be just as blessed as Mary. One of the most important ways we can minister to God is to humbly receive and believe his word like Mary did.

Indeed, Mary was a blessed woman. She was blessed because she ministered to God. She prayed. She heard his word and submitted to it. And then she literally ministered to Jesus Christ as he toddled on the earth and grew into a man.

In her intense devotion to God, Mary offered herself. She preferred God and his word over her reputation, security, future, or anything else. She was willing to go through shame, struggle, and hardship for his sake, even when she didn't understand.

And after Jesus' ascension, when the disciples gathered in the Upper Room, Mary was there, encouraging them, waiting for the Holy Spirit along with the rest. And as the early church grew, she helped the fledgling group grow so they could transform the world through the powerful kingdom of her Son.

There is a lot for us to learn from the life of Mary. But perhaps the greatest lesson that she teaches is that if someone, however small and insignificant, is willing to obey God's word through the offering of himself or herself, that person can become a vessel through whom God can come into the world and bring powerful transformation.

- Minister to Jesus -

1. Cultivate a meek and quiet spirit in order to find favor with God.

2. Always submit to God's word, even if his plans don't make sense according to your natural reasoning.

3. The Holy Spirit will bring God's word to pass. Don't take it into your own hands, but keep believing in God.

4. Be confident even in the midst of opposition. God's word will never fail.

- Prayer -

Heavenly Father, thank you for the precious gift of your Son. Help me humble myself under your mighty hand so I can experience your favor and see more of you in my life. Help me to accept your word, even when I don't understand how it will all work out. Increase my faith. Give me boldness. Help me to trust in you even when the way is hard, and let me never give up. Flood into me by your Holy Spirit and transform me into the person you want me to be. In Jesus' name I pray. Amen.

Part 2.

Mary Magdalene

Call upon me in the day of trouble; I will deliver you, and you will glorify me.

Psalm 50:15

MARY MAGDALENE IS MENTIONED at least twelve times in the New Testament, more than most apostles. She was an important disciple who was intimately involved in Jesus' ministry. The word disciple means student, and Jesus had both male and female students.

Mary Magdalene is often misunderstood. Centuries ago she was portrayed as a prostitute, even though the Bible never says that she was. Fiction writers today elaborate on these ancient theories, concocting blasphemous lies about Mary that go beyond accusations of prostitution. Such lies have spawned bestselling books and popular movies, as Satan swamps our culture with diabolical slander about Christ and his disciples.

These modern accusations are baseless. Jesus and his disciples were accused of all kinds of things by their enemies in ancient Palestine, but never of sexual immorality. To find the truth about Jesus, Mary Magdalene, or any of the other early disciples, we need to stick to the best historical reference book in the world - the Bible.

One of Satan's favorite weapons is slander. The very word *devil* means *slanderer*. Satan slanders people to destroy their reputations and sow confusion. The children of God must reject slander, not only about historical figures like Mary, but also about their neighbors and friends.

Captive in a Spiritual Fortress

Mary Magdalene is distinguished from other Marys by the name of her town, Magdala. Someone from Magdala was called a Magdalene. In the original language, *Magdala* means *fortress*.

The name of Mary's hometown that was appended to her name points out not only her natural origin, but her spiritual state. For much of Mary's life, she was imprisoned in a Satanic spiritual fortress - an invisible horror chamber - where she was tortured by seven strong demons which had possessed her (Mark 16:9).

These seven evil spirits would have made Mary's life miserable. The devil comes only to "steal, to kill, and to destroy" (John 10:10). Mary's health, mind, and body would have been under continual attack.

Mary's husband is never mentioned in the Bible. She probably never had a husband. But if she had been married once, it's likely that her husband divorced her after the demons came in.

In Magdala, Mary was probably known as the crazy woman, shunned by society, without family or friends to help her.

Mary might have tried ancient remedies like herbs, charms, or potions to get rid of her seven demons. Nothing worked. She was in a perpetual nightmare from which she could not awaken. Her mind and body must have been exhausted, worn out by raging evil.

Spiritual problems require spiritual solutions, and there is no answer to demonization except the power of God.

> Spiritual problems require spiritual solutions.

Freedom

One day Mary met Jesus.

The evil spirits inside Mary's body were shocked by the spiritual power of Jesus. They couldn't withstand his blaz-

49

ing spiritual light. They began writhing in pain. Maybe they shrieked through Mary's mouth. Maybe they contorted her body and threw her onto the ground. The Bible doesn't record the details of Mary's deliverance, but we can be sure it was remarkable.

Once Jesus cast a demon out of a man who was attending a synagogue meeting.

> Now in the synagogue there was a man who had a spirit of an unclean demon. And he cried out with a loud voice… But Jesus rebuked him, saying, "Be quiet, and come out of him!" And when the demon had thrown him in their midst, it came out of him and did not hurt him. (Luke 4:33-35)

Another time, Jesus cast out a demon that was particularly pernicious.

> "And wherever it seizes him, it throws him down; he foams at the mouth, gnashes his teeth, and becomes rigid…" And when he saw Him, immediately the spirit convulsed him, and he fell on the ground and wallowed, foaming at the mouth… He rebuked the unclean spirit, saying to it, "Deaf and dumb spirit, I command you, come out of him and enter him no more!" Then the spirit cried out, convulsed him greatly, and came out of him. And he became as one dead, so that many said, "He is dead." But Jesus took him by the hand and lifted him up, and he arose. (Mark 9:18-26)

Jesus cast out a lot of demons while upon the earth, revealing his supremacy over the devil. But Mary's deliverance was unique. The Bible mentions it twice, both times after the fact, as if for emphasis (Luke 8:2, Mark 16:9).

Jesus commanded the seven demons to get out of Mary Magdalene's body. In a moment, Satan's fortress was broken down. The demons ran away in fear.

Jesus is omnipotent. He can heal and deliver anyone. Anyone who is chained by the forces of evil can be set free. No case is too hard for the Lord. No demon can withstand the power of Jesus. Even today, the name of Jesus has power over all demons. Witchcraft is powerless against his name. Charms and spells are useless trifles against the Spirit of God. Jesus won the eternal victory against the devil and broke the power of Satan when he conquered death and rose up again. He has given authority to his children to cast out demons through the power of his name (Luke 10:19).

Mary was transformed. Her mind became quiet, free from taunting demonic voices. Her body, accustomed to the spasmodic reactions to the evil raging within her, was at rest. Her eyes and face were changed. Her posture and bearing were altered. Her personality was serene in comparison to its former tempest. Everything was at peace.

Mary was free! One touch from Jesus had changed her life. She had been lying down with dragons in their dark lairs, and now she was dancing with God in the fields of his pleasure!

Psalm 18 probably expresses Mary's condition and feelings after being delivered.

I will love you, O Lord, my strength.
The Lord is my rock my fortress and my deliverer;
My God, my strength, in whom I will trust;
My shield and the horn of my salvation, my stronghold.
I will call upon the Lord, who is worthy to be praised,
So shall I be saved from my enemies.
The pangs of death surrounded me;
And the floods of ungodliness made me afraid.
The sorrows of Sheol surrounded me;
The snares of death confronted me.
In my distress I called upon the Lord;
And cried out to my God;
He heard my voice from his temple,
And my cry came before him, even to his ears...
He sent from above, he took me;
He drew me out of many waters.
He delivered me from my strong enemy,
From those who hated me,
For they were too strong for me.
They confronted me in the day of my calamity,
But the Lord was my support.
He also brought me out into a broad place;
He delivered me because he delighted in me.

(Psalm 18:1-6, 16-19)

Our testimonies might not be as amazing as Mary's, but they are no less glorious. Every born-again believer has been set free by Jesus. Sin is a cruel master, and those held in its bondage are headed to hell. We can't free ourselves from these chains, and no one can free us but Christ.

"Therefore if the Son makes you free, you shall be free indeed" (John 8:36).

Jesus became Mary's refuge. He was a bulwark against the darkness and a protection from her enemies. She belonged to him now, and she had nothing more to fear.

If Mary ever felt threatened again by the devil, she was able to banish fear in Jesus' name. She probably felt she could face anything now. She had already been through hell.

A Close Disciple

After her deliverance, Mary's life took on a divine purpose. She attached herself to Jesus and his ministry. She accompanied him whenever and wherever she could. She began supporting him financially and in other ways. Mary began ministering to the one who had ministered so much to her.

> Now it came to pass, afterward, that He went through every city and village, preaching and bringing the glad tidings of the kingdom of God. And the twelve were

with Him, and certain women who had been healed of evil spirits and infirmities— Mary called Magdalene, out of whom had come seven demons, and Joanna the wife of Chuza, Herod's steward, and Susanna, and many others who provided for Him from their substance. (Luke 8:1-3)

Jesus needed help. He was in a position of both wealth and poverty at the same time. He had all the resources of heaven at his disposal, and yet he had real needs. He could create bread and fish out of thin air, but he was hungry and ate people's food. He was thirsty, and people gave him water. He was tired, and people gave him a bed to sleep on.

The humanity of Jesus gave Mary an opportunity to work with God in ministering redemption to the world. What a privilege it would have been to buy something for Jesus. How wonderful it would have been to spend money, time, or other resources on Christ! Mary Magdalene had this privilege, and she made the most of it. The heavenly riches that Jesus poured into Mary's life were translated back to him as an offering of service.

Mary must have thought, "He has done so much for me, how can I do anything less for him?"

Mary also knew there were many desperate people like her in the world. By ministering to Jesus, she was helping them find freedom.

Ministering to Jesus' Body Today

Jesus is in heaven now, but his body is still on the earth. Everyone who believes in Christ has become a part of him - "members of his body, of his flesh and of his bones" (Ephesians 5:30). This vast body is all over the world.

> As we minister to the body of Christ, we minister to God.

Jesus and his people are one. He identifies with them. When Saul (who became Paul) was persecuting the church, Jesus asked him why he was persecuting him (Acts 9:4). When the body of Christ suffers, Jesus suffers. Therefore, ministering to the body of Christ is like ministering to Jesus.

Today, God's people often struggle in this world. Some are hungry and need clothes. Some are languishing in prison, while others are sick. Jesus' body needs ministry. When we serve the body of Christ, giving them food or clothes, visiting those in prison, or praying for those who are sick, we are really serving Jesus.

"Assuredly, I say to you, inasmuch as you did it to one of the least of these my brethren, you did it to me" (Matt. 25:40).

We need to pray for each other. We need to bear each other's burdens. We need to love each other. As we minister to needs in the body of Christ, we minister to God.

Ministering to the body of Christ means supporting God's workers. If Jesus' ministry needed human support from people like Mary Magdalene, how much more will God's workers need support today?

Paul the apostle asked people to support him financially so they themselves could be blessed. "Not that I seek a gift, but I desire fruit that abounds to your account" (Philippians 4:17). Paul wasn't asking for money for his own selfish needs, but he wanted people to donate to his ministry so they could be blessed for eternity. Paul knew that if people gave to him, they were giving to God, and they were garnering for themselves eternal rewards.

Ministry Challenges

Ministry is not easy. As Mary traveled and ministered with Jesus, she encountered challenges. In those days, travel was hard. Jesus didn't stay at the best inns or demand the best food. He didn't even have his own donkey. He was willing to face challenges for the sake of his Father. He expected his followers to "endure hardness" (2 Tim. 2:3 KJV) too.

Following Jesus involves suffering. Jesus shined God's light in the midst of a world contaminated by the devil, and this light stirred up the darkness. Jesus was surrounded by spiritual war. He was constantly confronting the forces of darkness, battling demons, facing unbelief, and speaking against lies. Jesus stirred up controversy wherever he went, facing regular opposition from religious and governmental leaders. Salvation didn't come cheap. As Mary accompanied Jesus, she shared in these hardships.

If we're going to represent Jesus to the world, we must take up our cross. Following Jesus is not about being blessed by God with a lot of money and earthly success. It's about us blessing God and following in the footsteps of Jesus. That may mean facing hardship.

The End

As the days went on, Mary could sense that trouble was brewing. The leaders of Israel seemed increasingly resistant to Jesus. Though some recognized Jesus was the Messiah, others were becoming increasingly hostile.

Suddenly, Jesus was attacked by a mob and arrested. He was dragged to a sham trial.

Mary Magdalene was likely stunned. She probably didn't expect things to move so fast.

A few days earlier, people were flocking to Jesus for healing. Now they were either mocking him or running away. People can be very fickle. Even Jesus' closest friends left him. Peter denied knowing him, frightened of the repercussions that might come upon him if he were associated with Jesus of Nazareth.

"I will strike the shepherd, and the sheep of the flock will be scattered" (Matt. 26:31b).

Maybe the next time Mary Magdalene saw Jesus, he was being forced to walk to the place of execution. Battered and bloody, Jesus struggled along the road to Golgotha, carrying a huge cross.

Mary probably wondered how this could be happening.

Most onlookers thought Jesus was a terrible criminal. They didn't have time to delve into all the details about his case. In their minds, his disciples were probably guilty too.

Mary Magdalene didn't care what they thought. At one point, they thought she was crazy. Why would it matter what they thought now? If Jesus had to go to the cross, so would she. Mary didn't mind being seen with Jesus, even in the worst places. Taking up our cross and following Jesus can be shockingly hard. Follow him anyway.

At the Foot of the Cross

Mary Magdalene joined Mary, his mother, at the foot of the cross (John 19:25).

Together, they saw the soldiers nail him to wooden beams. They watched as his body was hoisted up between earth and heaven, pain slashing through every corner of his flesh like a thousand knives.

Mary Magdalene gasped as her spiritual fortress was broken down. Christ, her tower of light, was being ravaged by

Satan, her former dark captor. It looked like hell's payback time.

Old fears might have crept back into her heart. She might have wondered if Satan could kill Jesus, what could he do to her? If her strong tower was knocked down, where would she find refuge?

Mary Magdalene shuddered.

These two Marys may have huddled together as tremendous sorrow coursed through them. They were in anguish as Jesus struggled against death, each breath becoming harder than the one before.

He looked down at them through blurry eyes. He was dazed, but at the beginning of his crucifixion, he could see them standing there. He seemed to have nothing to offer them now. They weren't there at the cross for their sakes. They were there for *his* sake.

Their presence at his darkest hour must have ministered to him. Someone was there. Someone cared. Someone loved him. Not everyone had left him. The presence of Mary Magdalene and his Mother probably gave Jesus comfort as the terrible weight of the sins of the world bore down on his shoulders, chasing the life from his body.

Jesus cried out once more. God no longer seemed to hear or care. His Father had turned his face away and could no longer look at his Son. Jesus became sin for us.

The eternal Christ breathed his last breath and died. The strong, invincible Messiah had been slain.

The two Marys probably held each other, shaking, understanding each other perhaps like no one else in this darkest moment of history.

The future seemed bleak. Hopeless. How could they survive in this hostile world without him?

His mission seemed a failure.

The soldiers ran a sword through his side. The sun went black at midday. The world became dark.

His mother stumbled away, overwhelmed, unable to take any more.

Going Further

Mary Magdalene stayed.

She saw them take his body down from the cross. She saw them pry his dead hands and feet loose from those iron nails. She must have been numb now, past feeling.

Mary forced herself onward.

Right before the crucifixion, in the Garden of Gethsemane, when Jesus was agonizing in prayer, he didn't give up. He went forward and prayed more earnestly (Matthew 26:39, Luke 22:44).

Mary Magdalene went further too.

Mary followed Jesus' body to the tomb. She was there when he was buried (Mark 15:47). She still wanted to be with him. She didn't want to leave him. She had been with him throughout his ministry, whenever and wherever she could. She wasn't going to leave him now.

The stone was rolled over the cave where his body lay. Finally, the cruel grave had separated Mary Magdalene from Jesus.

Soldiers came. Maybe they roughly told her to leave.

Weak, helpless, and confused, Mary tore herself from the cemetery. She staggered away, her heart broken, her mind a blur, her face wet with grief.

Waiting

Back home, amidst sorrow's stupor, Mary prepared spices to embalm Jesus' dead body (Mark 16:1). This was a ritual that any dead person was entitled to, but for Mary, it was much more than a rite. It was a final opportunity to show respect and love to the One who had done so much for her. It also meant preservation. Mary wanted to preserve Jesus. Bodies rot in graves, but these spices would help his body remain intact a little longer. Mary wanted to fight with Jesus against the power of the grave.

The Sabbath dawned. Mary was stuck at home. She couldn't go to the tomb. Maybe Mary remembered how Jesus had often faced difficulties on the Sabbath. The religious leaders often seemed to be arguing with him on that day. He healed people, and the Pharisees got so mad. It was their holy day! Shouldn't they be kinder, at least on that day? Mary wanted to go and minister to Jesus' dead body that Sabbath day. She wanted to cover his body with her precious spices. But she knew that if the Pharisees found her wandering around and embalming a dead body on the Sabbath, they would get mad at her too. Now it wasn't just the grave that was separating her from Jesus. It was dead religion.

Dawn

Mary didn't sleep much that Sabbath night. She didn't wait for the sun to rise. While it was still dark, she ran to the tomb with her spices (John 20:1).

She was the first disciple to get there. What she saw shocked her. The stone had been rolled away. Christ's body was not there!

She ran back frantically to tell the others. After hearing her report, they came and looked for themselves. They went back home, wondering.

Mary stayed at the tomb. She didn't want to leave. She was weeping (John 20:11). She couldn't understand why someone had opened the tomb and taken his body away.

A man approached her. She looked through her tears briefly at his form and looked away. She thought that he was the cemetery gardener. She assumed that he took Jesus' body and put it somewhere. (John 20:14-17.)

The man asked her why she was crying. She said she just wanted to know where his body was.

The man replied, "Mary".

Instantly, the familiar voice told Mary that the "gardener" was Jesus.

He was alive!

"Now when he rose early on the first day of the week, he appeared first to Mary Magdalene, out of whom he had cast seven demons" (Mark 16:9).

Mary was the first disciple to see the risen Lord Jesus.

A cataclysm of emotion seized her. Her Lord had won! He had conquered death! She reached out and tried to hold onto her triumphant God.

Jesus told her that she must not touch him now. She had to go tell the others. They needed to know that he was alive.

Sharing the Revelation

Revelation brings responsibility. Those with revelation are not meant to keep it to themselves, but get it out to others.

Mary again had to leave Jesus. She didn't want to, but she knew that obedience to Jesus is more important than just enjoying his presence.

Maybe it wasn't easy for Mary to go tell Peter and the others. After all, she had a checkered past and might not be trusted. But Jesus commissioned Mary to testify of him because he loved her. He wanted her to be healed in all aspects of her life, including socially. He wanted his disciples to see her as valuable, as God saw her. A person's past does not necessarily define who they are now, especially after Jesus has intervened.

"She went and told those who had been with him, as they mourned and wept. And when they heard that he was alive and had been seen by her, they did not believe" (Mark 16:10-11).

The other disciples didn't believe Mary when she told them Jesus was alive. Maybe they thought she had gone crazy again.

But Mary spoke the truth.

Soon, the disciples saw Jesus for themselves, and her testimony was confirmed. They probably had new respect for Mary.

Attachment Discipleship

Mary Magdalene - the formerly crazed, demonized woman, who was attached to Jesus possibly like no other disciple - was the first to see him after his resurrection. This was an awesome privilege. Mary had longed to be with Jesus, possibly more than any other disciple, and she was rewarded. Those who long for Jesus are going to see him.

Mary knew the love of God, and this set her free from fear. "Perfect love casts out fear" (1 John 4:18b). Free from fear, she could "follow the Lamb wherever he goes" (Rev. 14:4b).

Throughout Jesus' ministry, Mary was there. She ministered to his practical needs and to the needs of his disciples. And in the end when the other disciples ran away, Mary stayed. She followed him to the cross and then to the tomb. And Mary was the first disciple to see Jesus after he conquered death. Her attachment to Jesus prompted him to bless her with a special revelation of his resurrected glory, before anyone else.

- Minister to Jesus -

1. Jesus has rescued you from Satan, sin, and hell. Jesus has the power to deliver anyone!

2. No one is more worthy of your time, attention, and effort than Jesus. Follow him wherever he leads you.

3. Recognize the needs of your fellow believers and meet those needs. As you do, you minister to Jesus.

4. God wants you to share with others what he has taught you.

- *Prayer* -

Father, praise you for your complete and eternal victory over Satan. Thank you for delivering me from sin, evil, and the powers of darkness. My life now belongs to you, because you bought me with your blood. Please help me to stay close to you and follow you wherever you go. Open my eyes to see the needs of your people around me, so I can meet those needs. Help me to minister to your body. Grant me a fresh revelation of Jesus, in whose name I pray. Amen.

Part 3.

Mary of Bethany

I beseech you therefore, brethren, by the mercies of God, that you present your bodies a living sacrifice, holy, acceptable to God, which is your reasonable service.

Romans 12:1

CHRIST STOOD at the door of the grave of a dead man and shouted, "Lazarus, come forth!"

A rotting, stinking corpse woke up and tottered out of a tomb in front of a large crowd. Lazarus was brought forth by the power of Jesus' word, and then he just stood there - the form of a human body covered in a mass of tight bandages covering his face and body. Everyone was too shocked to do anything. This is the kind of thing that gives Satan nightmares.

People finally unwrapped the cloths and freed Lazarus, and there he was - alive - with no stench of death upon him. Everyone was astounded. This miracle almost put people out of their minds.

The resurrection of Lazarus was remarkable, chosen by God to bless a special family. Jesus loved Lazarus and his sisters Mary and Martha (John 11:5). That's why he orchestrated events so that this awesome miracle could happen.

There was something unique about this family. Jesus spent a lot of time at their house, not because they needed his help and had so many problems, but because he liked to be there. Something about them touched his heart.

Come Lord Jesus, Be Our Guest

Now it happened as they went that He entered a certain village; and a certain woman named Martha welcomed Him into her house. And she had a sister called Mary, who also sat at Jesus' feet and heard His word. But Martha was distracted with much serving, and she approached Him and said, "Lord, do You not care that my sister has left me to serve alone? Therefore tell her to help me." And Jesus answered and said to her, "Martha, Martha, you are worried and troubled about many things. But one thing is needed, and Mary has chosen that good part, which will not be taken away from her." (Luke 10:38-41)

The first time Jesus met this family, he came over to their house for dinner. Hospitality was important in those days, and hospitality to the Messiah was especially important. Hospitality means sacrificing so that guests can be comfortable, and the more important a guest is, the greater the sacrifice should be.

Being hospitable to Jesus was not easy. He was the most important person who ever lived, worthy of the best hospitality. Not only that, he had many disciples traveling with him, and hosting so many people would have been hard. There were few conveniences in those days. Cooking for an ordinary family took a lot of time, but with a dozen or so more people added to the mix, it was even harder.

We join the scene right before mealtime.

The household was busy. In those days, whenever a meal was being prepared, it was "all hands on deck" - at least all the female hands. The two sisters, Martha and Mary, were supposed to do most of the work. Martha was busy fulfilling the duties of what would have been expected of a hostess: cooking, cleaning, and getting everything ready for dinner. She was bustling about, frantic at the last moment, throwing things together for this large group of important people who had come over to eat.

Martha's activity seemed appropriate. Guests meant work. They had to be made comfortable. Culture defined such interactions, and social norms required conformance.

Martha saw her sister Mary sitting around. Martha was annoyed. Why wasn't Mary helping? There was so much to do! The bread wasn't baked, the peas weren't boiled, and the meat needed cooking! Martha probably didn't blurt out her frustration immediately, but resentment simmered in her heart.

Soon, Martha couldn't take it anymore. She erupted. She scolded Mary in front of everyone. She even reproached Jesus. "Lord, do You not care that my sister has left me to serve alone? Therefore tell her to help me!" (Luke 10:40).

Martha was sure that Jesus would be on her side. She thought he must be tired after a long day of ministering to others. What man wouldn't like some good, hot food at the end of a long day? Jesus was worthy of being served! We must serve God! Martha was sure that Jesus would vindicate her and put Mary in her place.

But Jesus corrected Martha instead. "Martha, Martha. You are worried and upset about many things, but Mary has chosen that good part that shall not be taken away from her" (Luke 10:41-42).

Jesus or Ministry?

Martha was a busy woman. She wasn't working for herself, getting her own dinner ready. She had to work for Jesus! She had to minister to him and his disciples, and she was trying to bless God! That was impressive perhaps, but in the process of all her activity *for* Jesus, she was missing out on Jesus himself.

We must minister *to* Jesus before ministering *for* Jesus. Ministering *to* Jesus is what really matters. It's true that there are a lot of things that need to be done in the world, and many "Christian" concerns vie for our time and attention. But in our zeal to serve Jesus, we need to be careful that we're not missing out on what really matters.

> Don't allow ministry for Jesus take you away from ministry to Jesus.

Martha's ministry did not originate in God; it was based on her own mind. She thought she knew what Jesus wanted and that she had figured out how to serve God. She was wrong. We can't serve Jesus according to what we think is right. We need to be led by his Spirit.

Manmade ministry is a burden. Jesus said Martha was "cumbered." Her service had become heavy. Her ministry was damaging her relationships with God and with other people. It was also hurting herself, turning her into an anxious and troubled mess.

> Come to me, all who labor and are heavy laden, and I will give you rest. Take my yoke upon you and learn from me, for I am gentle and lowly in heart, and you will find rest for your souls. For my yoke is easy and my burden is light. (Matt. 11:28-30)

Jesus doesn't want us to be overloaded and stressed out. His yoke is not hard. It's easy, because it draws us close to him.

Wait

It's often better to wait than to work. The first disciples had to wait in the Upper Room for the outpouring of the Holy Spirit before they could really accomplish anything for God. They didn't rush out into Jerusalem armed with their own ideas about how to do ministry. They didn't try a lot of things hoping something would work out. They waited patiently until God fulfilled his promise. Then he faithfully poured out his Holy Spirit, filling them with power from on High. Then they did what he wanted them to do, in his power, and he was glorified.

It's not always easy to wait. The world values activity and production, and the Christian world values working for God. There are a lot of Marthas in the church who think they know what needs to be done, and they raise an eyebrow at those who don't join them in their service.

They say, "Why aren't you doing anything? Don't you see all the things that need to be done? Just plug in somewhere and do something for God!"

It's true that we're living in urgent times and there is much to be done for the Lord. But we are called to hear from God and specifically do what he wants us to do.

Activity in and of itself is no virtue. We don't need to be busy just to be busy. The Lord's kingdom can only come in God's way, in God's time, and it can only come when we actually hear from God and do what he says. It's not enough for us to just do things according to our own thoughts and plans. We have to learn spiritual precision.

We must halt our own activity if we're going to hear God speak to us. It is possible to do a lot of ministry and be very active serving God - but if we don't actually hear the words of the Savior, all our work might be for nothing. Jesus must guide and lead all ministry that will be of eternal consequence. We need

> It's often better to wait than to work.

to wait. We need to listen. We need to stop like Mary did. This might upset a few Marthas, but we need to hear from God.

Waiting on God is the secret of our strength. Isaiah said:

> Those who wait on the Lord shall renew their strength; they shall mount up with wings like eagles, they shall run and not be weary, they shall walk and not faint. (Isaiah 40:31)

When we wait, we can receive instructions from God and be filled with the Holy Spirit. Then when we act, God will work through us, and there will be supernatural results.

Listen

While Martha was running around getting hot bread out of the oven, Mary was doing something more important. God was sitting in her house, ministering his word! Mary was busy grabbing as much fresh, heavenly bread from Jesus' lips as she could. She knew that when Jesus shows up, he takes precedence over everything else. The living bread coming out of Jesus' mouth was more valuable to her than the material bread which had sent Martha into such a panic.

Mary valued the words of Jesus. He spoke words of Spirit and Life - words that blessed her like nothing else. As he spoke, releasing heaven into that room, living water washed over her soul. Mary felt more alive than ever.

As she received Jesus' words, she was not only feeding her own soul, she was ministering to Jesus. Jesus was glad when someone like Mary valued his words enough to lay aside their ordinary obligations and listen.

As Mary received the word of God with humility and understanding, she was *worshiping*.

Jesus wants us to hear and understand what he's saying. When we quiet ourselves from the bustle of life and leave the cares of the world behind just to hear from him, we are not only blessed with revelation from heaven, we honor God. We show him that he is more important to us than anything else.

Jesus said, "One thing is necessary." That *one thing* is to hear from God. True disciples sit at the feet of Jesus, with their ears in tune with him.

Sit

> Hearing from God is the beginning of true ministry.

Mary sat. Sitting sounds easy, but it's often not. Mary had to face the wrath of her sister and the scowls of others who probably thought she was lazy and irresponsible. But Mary sat anyway. She was more motivated by devotion to Jesus than by the fear of man.

Sitting is spiritually powerful, because it symbolizes rest. When Jesus finished his work on the earth, he rose up into heaven and *sat* on the right hand of God. Sitting symbolized that his work in redeeming the world was over. Jesus calls us to sit and rest with him.

Mary sat, showing that she had stopped her own work. She had found rest in Jesus' presence. In the midst of the noise, judgments, and worries of those around her, Mary sat down and heard from God.

To hear the words of Jesus for our own lives, we need to quiet ourselves. We need to lay aside our own activities.

"He who has entered into his rest has himself also ceased from his works as God did from his" (Hebrews 4:10).

Sitting and waiting for Jesus to speak is not wasting our lives. A wasted life starts with doing a lot of things God never told us to do.

Outside the Box

Mary just sat there with the Messiah. She was no brazen, immoral woman. She was just a simple woman who cared more about Jesus than she did about herself. She knew that her identity was not based on what people thought about her, but on what Jesus said. She didn't need to preserve her reputation in the eyes of people. Let all that go, as long as she was able to sit next to God.

Mary was not an outsider. She wasn't a shy eavesdropper peeking her head through the doorway. She was right there in the middle of it all, sitting next to the main man.

Mary was unashamed to be close to Jesus in front of everyone. Let us be bold like Mary. Don't worry about what anyone says. It doesn't matter what they think or say. Our eternal reputation is settled by God. Love God in front of the world!

Mary accepted the reality of her position in Christ.

> A true disciple honors Jesus above culture. He or she is not hindered by the judgments of others.

The fact that she was sitting right next to Jesus shows that she was one of his closest disciples.

"All that the Father gives me will come to me; and the one who comes to me I will by no means cast out" (John 6:37).

At His Feet

Mary was sitting at Christ's feet. This means she trusted him. She wasn't afraid of him.

> There is no fear in love. But perfect love drives out fear, because fear has to do with punishment. The one who fears is not made perfect in love. (1 John 4:18)

Jesus tells us to become like little children. "Unless you change and become like little children, you will never enter the kingdom of heaven" (Matt. 18:3).

Children trust implicitly. They are free to love and be loved. Mary was submitting, listening, and understanding Jesus. The word of God comes to the lowly in heart, not to the high and mighty. Knowing God's love enabled Mary to come close to Jesus and hear God's word.

By listening to Jesus and valuing him above herself, her family, and her society, Mary ministered to Jesus much more effectively than if she had served him a plate of hot peas and buns.

But Mary wasn't done. She was going to minister to Jesus in an even more powerful way later.

MARY ANOINTS CHRIST

"THEN, SIX DAYS before the Passover, Jesus came to Bethany, where Lazarus was who had been dead, whom He had raised from the dead. There they made Him a supper; and Martha served, but Lazarus was one of those who sat at the table with Him" (John 12:1-2).

About a week before his crucifixion, Jesus returned to Mary's town, Bethany. He knew that he was approaching the end of his earthly ministry, and that death awaited him in Jerusalem. Maybe he was at Bethany in order to find some encouragement before the power of darkness struck him.

Jesus went to Bethany six days before the Passover, according to John. The gospels record that he spent much of his final week in Bethany before the crucifixion, going to Jerusalem during the day, teaching in the temple, and returning to Bethany at night.

Then, two days before the Passover, Mary and her family made a supper for Jesus in Bethany (Matthew 26:1-14, and Mark 14:1-9).

Lazarus was there. In this familiar scene, Martha was busy serving again.

And at this supper, just two days before the Passover, Mary shocked everyone again.

"Then Mary took a pound of very costly oil of spikenard, anointed the feet of Jesus, and wiped his feet with her hair" (John 12:3a).

If Martha didn't understand her sister back then, she probably really didn't understand her now.

Matthew wrote about the same event:

> And when Jesus was in Bethany at the house of Simon the leper, a woman came to Him having an alabaster flask of very costly fragrant oil, and she poured it on His head as He sat at the table. (Matt 26:6-7)

Simon the Leper was probably either Lazarus' father or Martha's husband. He was probably healed earlier from leprosy, probably by Jesus, which is why he is called "the leper" - remembered by his former condition. "The woman" was Mary, as we learn from John 12:3.

Mary had an alabaster box - a stone jar - full of expensive perfume. It was worth over 300 denarii (Mark 14:5). Since one denarius was one day's wage (Matt. 20:2), this was one year's wages - approximately $40,000 in today's money.

This perfume had probably come from a remote area in the Himalayan mountains.

In those days, it's possible that young women had vials of expensive perfume as security, an asset to bank on if their lives ever faced uncertainty. For example, another woman poured out a jar of perfume on Jesus in Luke 7:36-38. This is a different event that happened earlier, with a different woman, in a different town, in a different house.

Mary's alabaster jar of perfume was probably the most valuable thing she had.

In front of everyone, Mary took out her alabaster box, broke it, and poured out all the perfume on Jesus.

"The house was filled with the fragrance of the oil" (John 12:3b).

It was a strong perfume, and the smell invaded the house. Perfume is meant to be used in small doses, and a little perfume goes a long way, but Mary poured out the whole jar on Jesus!

Mary wasn't shy. She didn't care what people thought about her. She rubbed the perfume onto Jesus in front of everyone. She poured it on his head (Mark 14:3). From there it went onto his clothes and over his body. Then she poured some more perfume on his feet and rubbed his feet with her long hair (John 12:3). She wanted her perfume to stick to Jesus.

Opposition

The disciples became upset:

> But when His disciples saw it, they were indignant, say-
> ing, "Why this waste? For this fragrant oil might have
> been sold for much and given to the poor." (Matt. 26:8-
> 9)

Mary again faced criticism for her devotion to God. This
time it wasn't her sister scolding her, it was Jesus' own disciples. Jesus' disciples thought the perfume shouldn't have
been wasted like this on Jesus, but should have been sold
instead.

This act of devotion deeply touched Jesus' heart, but his
disciples didn't understand why. They had no idea why
Mary had done this. They didn't appreciate the things that
were so precious to Jesus.

Jesus quickly defended Mary. "You have the poor with you
always, but me you do not have always" (Matt. 26:11). Ministering to the poor is good, but ministering to Jesus is even
better.

Jesus told everyone, "Wherever this gospel is preached in
the whole world, what this woman has done will be told as
a memorial for her" (Mark 14:9). Through her perfume
offering, Mary obtained a testimony that would be remembered throughout history.

What was so special about Mary's act? Was it special because she gave up such a valuable possession for God? No. Others gave up more for Jesus, but they didn't obtain such a lasting testimony. Mary's perfume offering was about more than sacrificial giving.

The Disciples Didn't Understand

In a couple of days, Jesus was about to face the biggest challenge any person had ever faced in the history of the world. Every sin that had ever been committed by anyone was about to be laid on his back. When the Passover lambs were to be killed throughout Israel, and their blood was going to flow like streams into the gutters, Jesus was going to be slain for the sins of the whole world. He was going to taste death for every person who ever lived.

Jesus often told his disciples what he was about to go through, but they didn't understand.

> "Let these words sink down into your ears, for the Son of Man is about to be betrayed into the hands of men." But they did not understand this saying, and it was hidden from them so that they did not perceive it; and they were afraid to ask Him about this saying. (Luke 9:44-45)

Jesus tried explaining it to them again.

> Then He took the twelve aside and said to them, "Behold, we are going up to Jerusalem, and all things that

> are written by the prophets concerning the Son of Man
> will be accomplished. For He will be delivered to the
> Gentiles and will be mocked and insulted and spit
> upon. They will scourge Him and kill Him. And the
> third day He will rise again." But they understood none
> of these things; this saying was hidden from them, and
> they did not know the things which were spoken.
> (Luke 18:31b-34)

Jesus plainly explained to his disciples that he was going to be arrested, beaten, and killed. They just didn't understand. Maybe the word of God didn't fit into their theology, so they rejected it.

> From that time Jesus began to show to His disciples
> that He must go to Jerusalem, and suffer many things
> from the elders and chief priests and scribes, and be
> killed, and be raised the third day. Then Peter took
> Him aside and began to rebuke Him, saying, "Far be it
> from You, Lord; this shall not happen to You!" But He
> turned and said to Peter, "Get behind Me, Satan! You
> are an offense to Me, for you are not mindful of the
> things of God, but the things of men." (Matt. 16:21-23)

This time, not only did Peter not understand the necessity of Christ's death, but he discouraged him from going to the cross. He declared that such a plan was wrong.

Satan was speaking through Peter, trying to discourage Jesus from taking away the sins of the world.

Jesus was human. In the midst of his darkest hour, he wanted someone to understand him and sympathize with him. He didn't want to be all alone. But his disciples were unable to have compassion on him because they couldn't understand him.

"I looked for someone to take pity, but there was none; and for comforters, but I found none" (Ps. 69:20b).

Mary Understood

But one woman understood. She believed Jesus when he said he was about to suffer. She understood him when he said he would be beaten. She knew that he was about to die. That is why she got out her alabaster jar. Mary poured the perfume on Jesus for the day of his death.

"For in pouring this fragrant oil on My body, she did it for my burial" (Matt. 26:12).

Mary seemed to know that if she anointed Jesus at that time, the smell of the perfume would remain on his body until he was buried. And according to Jesus, she was right.

"Let her alone; she has kept this for the day of my burial" (John 12:7)

Ancient perfumes were long-lasting. They were used in lieu of regular baths and meant to cover other odors. Mary probably hoped her perfume would remain potent on Jesus' body until his body was buried in the grave.

Mary was moving prophetically when she anointed Jesus. She was led by the Holy Spirit.

Jesus' head was about to be pierced by thorns and beaten with rods. Mary poured oil on his head. His body was about to be lashed, and his flesh was going to turn bloody and blue. Mary poured oil on his body. His feet were about to be pierced by rough iron nails. Mary poured oil on his feet and rubbed the oil into his skin with her hair.

While Mary was sitting at Jesus' feet months earlier, she was really *listening* to him. That's why she knew what he was about to endure, even when others couldn't understand. It's why she got out her perfume and poured out her worship.

Jesus went from Bethany, anointed by Mary, to face the devil.

The next evening was the Last Supper. Jesus sat for a final meal with his disciples. Out of this final fellowship, Judas Iscariot slipped into the dark night to betray Christ to the government. Jesus went from the Last Supper to the garden of Gethsemane. There an intense spiritual war began. Christ prayed in agony with great drops of blood flowing down his face. He had brought his disciples along, hoping they would pray with him and be a source of encouragement; but they all fell asleep, a source of sorrow instead. Their sleepiness on the brink of his murder emphasized that they didn't understand or seem to care about his impending horror.

But the smell of Mary's perfume, applied just the day before, probably lingered on Jesus' clothes, on his hair, on his body, reminding him that someone understood him. Someone cared.

Jesus was attacked by an angry, armed mob. He was dragged before the government and handed over to hardened soldiers. They spat on his face and beat him until pieces of skin hung off his body. His closest disciples denied ever knowing him. Even Peter rejected him. The physical and emotional turmoil that Jesus went through was excruciating. Through it all, Jesus probably still smelled Mary's perfume.

Smell is one of the most powerful triggers of memory and emotion. "Human behavior is strongly influenced by olfaction. Environmental odors can prime specific memories and emotions, influence autonomic nervous system activation, [and] shape perceptions of stress" (McGann, *Science*, 12 May 2017). Smell is powerful.

Blind and deaf Helen Keller said, "Smell...transports you across thousands of miles and all the years you have lived... It recalls in a flash entire epochs of our dearest experience" (Keller, *The World I Live In*).

The scent of Mary's perfume would have helped Jesus remember the good things, the intimate fellowship, and true love among his disciples - even when he was going through hell.

Nails pierced his flesh as he was nailed to the cross. Hanging there naked, exposed to the world, under the weight of all its terrible sins, there seemed to be no one left. His friends had all run away. The other Marys - his Mother and Mary Magdalene - were at the foot of his cross, but as the pangs of death came upon him and blurred his eyes, it's likely he could no longer see them.

But Mary of Bethany was still there in spirit, in perhaps a more profound way than the others. The smell of her perfume may have brought back to his mind memories of comfort, of pleasantness. It probably wafted up from his beard, from his body. Until he breathed his last, even when he could no longer see, he could still smell. It's possible that Mary's perfume was the only earthly comfort he had left, even after God forsook him.

Through her precious perfume, Mary ministered to Jesus in the most profound way possible. This perfume seems to have encouraged him all the way to the end, until his last breath.

Even then, Mary's perfume accompanied Jesus to the grave, fulfilling its purpose, for Mary had anointed him for his burial.

Three days later, he rose up again.

"Who is this coming out of the wilderness like pillars of smoke, perfumed with myrrh and frankincense, with all the merchant's fragrant powders?" (Song of Solomon 3:6).

It's no wonder that Jesus said that whenever the gospel is told, the powerful testimony of Mary at Bethany anointing him with perfume would be told along with it.

- *Minister to Jesus* -

1. Don't be busy just to be busy, but take time for God and his word.

2. Make sure your Christian service is based on God's word and not on your own thoughts or on the thoughts of others.

3. Be willing to wait until you hear specifically from God before rushing ahead.

4. Whatever you give up for the sake of Jesus will be worth it.

5. Be close to Jesus in front of the world.

6. Look for how you can encourage other believers who are facing challenges.

- *Prayer* -

Heavenly Father, I want to serve you in a way that pleases you, and not just in a way that I think is right. Remove from me any wrong thoughts I have about you. Cause your word to shape my thinking. Forgive me for all the things I have done when I thought I was serving you but were not led by your Spirit. I know that your ways are much better than my ways. I don't want to run off on my own and waste my life with useless activity. Please lead me by your Holy Spirit. In Jesus' name I pray. Amen.

Part 4.

The Bride

You are all fair, my love, and there is no spot in you.

Song of Solomon 4:7

THE THREE MARYS LIVED in a religious culture. In their time, the Bible and God-talk were central to just about everything. But when God showed up, most of the religious people rejected him. More precisely, they hated him and crucified him. The cross shows that Jesus and religion are very, very different.

Jesus wants us to understand him. He wants us to love him. Many people today say they love Jesus, but they don't listen to him. They run around doing religious things, but they ignore Jesus himself. Sometimes religious people get busy - too busy to hear the voice of God.

Jesus wants us to hear what he's saying and leave our own ways behind. We don't need to do a bunch of great things in order to get God's appreciation. We need to sit at his feet and hear his word. If we can understand what God is saying and respond in love, it will mean more to him than anything else. Hearing and understanding God's word is the starting point for ministering to Jesus.

Jesus' Bride

At the end of history, a group of disciples will touch Jesus' heart. They will leave empty Christianity behind and encounter the reality of God. They will not be a denomination or an organization. They will be a spiritual body of people that follow the Lamb wherever he goes, submitting to whatever he says, and worshipping him "in Spirit and Truth" (John 4:24b). This anointed group of disciples will be the bride of Jesus Christ.

Jesus didn't get married to any woman while he walked the earth. He died and rose up to heaven as a bachelor. That's because he was looking to marry a corporate bride comprised of people all over the world who are totally devoted to him. Someday Jesus will have his wife.

This bride is going to get ready to be married to Jesus soon. The invitation is going forth from the Holy Spirit, calling people to complete dedication to God.

"Blessed are those who are called to the marriage supper of the Lamb!" (Rev. 19:9b).

What could be better than becoming the spouse of God? There is no higher calling!

Sadly, not many people will be willing to become the bride of Christ. This is because they love other things too much.

> The kingdom of heaven is like a certain king who arranged a marriage for his son, and sent out his servants to call those who were invited to the wedding; and they were not willing to come. (Matthew 22:2-3)

Those who refused to come to the wedding supper were too busy with their own things that they didn't want to become the bride of Christ. They put their businesses, their families, and their pursuit of money ahead of God.

> But they all with one accord began to make excuses. The first said to him, 'I have bought a piece of ground, and I must go and see it. I ask you to have me excused.' And another said, 'I have bought five yoke of oxen, and I am going to test them. I ask you to have me excused.' Still another said, 'I have married a wife, and therefore I cannot come' (Luke 14:18-20).

Only those Christians who are willing to make sacrifices will become the bride of Christ.

> There are sixty queens and eighty concubines, and virgins without number. My dove, my perfect one, is the

only one, the only one of her mother, the favorite of the one who bore her. (Song of Solomon 6:8-9)

There are many denominations and churches in the world today which serve over 2 billion Christians. But only a remnant of these will become the bride of Jesus Christ.

Preparing the Bride

For those that can hear God's voice, it's time to get ready for Jesus. Preparation happens through submission to the word of God. God is preparing his bride to be one with him through his word.

> That He might sanctify and cleanse her with the washing of water by the word, that He might present her to Himself a glorious church, not having spot or wrinkle or any such thing, but that she should be holy and without blemish. (Ephesians 5:26-27)

As we apply the word of God to our lives, we are cleansed by its pure spiritual water. As the word of God washes over us as divine waves from heaven, it delivers us from evil and shapes us according to God.

We need to abandon the religious ways of man and accept the word of God. No matter what God tells us to do, we need to do it. We must not consider it too hard, radical, or extreme. We need to submit to Jesus, not only individually, but corporately. As we give up our own ways to follow

God's ways, we will begin to be revealed on the earth as the glorious bride of Christ.

Getting Ready for Jesus

The three Marys show us what the bride of Christ is going to be like.

Like Mary of Bethany, she will sit at Jesus' feet and hear his word. We must leave our own activities behind so we can understand what Jesus is saying. We must cut through vain religion and social obligation and understand the heart of God. When we understand his word, we must be willing to give up everything for him as we respond in humble devotion.

> Your words were found, and I ate them, and Your word was to me the joy and rejoicing of my heart; for I am called by Your name, O Lord God of hosts. (Jeremiah 15:16)

Like Mary Magdalene, the bride of Christ will long for Jesus above all else. We must be attached to Jesus, unable to let him go. We must follow him wherever he leads, being attentive to the needs of his body, supporting his ministers. As we stay close to Jesus, we will meet him in ways that others don't and see him before others do.

> These are the ones who were not defiled with women, for they are virgins. These are the ones who follow the Lamb wherever He goes. These were redeemed from

among men, being firstfruits to God and to the Lamb. (Revelation 14:4)

Like Mary his mother, the bride of Christ will be willing to obey God's word, even if it costs us our own reputation or life. We must be willing to say yes to God with meekness and humility, even when we don't understand all the implications of obedience. We must become willing vessels for the Spirit of God to flow through so we can release deliverance into the earth.

Jesus is ready. He's waiting for us more than we're waiting for him.

Marriage Supper of the Lamb

When the bride of Christ is ready, she's going to meet Jesus.

> "Let us be glad and rejoice and give Him glory, for the marriage of the Lamb has come, and His wife has made herself ready." And to her it was granted to be arrayed in fine linen, clean and bright, for the fine linen is the righteous acts of the saints. Then he said to me, "Write: 'Blessed are those who are called to the marriage supper of the Lamb!'" (Revelation 19:7-8)

When the bride of Christ is ready, there's going to be a great spiritual feast - the marriage supper of the Lamb. Those who are part of the remnant group of faithful disciples are going to sit at the table like a queen - as a bride adorned for her husband. At that time, Jesus and his church will become one. The disciples will be filled with God. The world will be astounded by the revelation of power and glory that will be revealed into the earth through the union of Christ and his bride.

"Then I, John, saw the holy city, New Jerusalem, coming down out of heaven from God, prepared as a bride adorned for her husband" (Revelation 21:2).

Shut Out

When Christ and his bride sit down together and feast at the wedding supper of the Lamb, the door into this possibility will shut. Many professing Christians will be shut out. They thought they were living for Jesus on the earth and serving him, but they will be unable to get into this great feast. They won't be able to be part of the bride.

> The bridegroom came, and those who were ready went in with him to the wedding; and the door was shut. Afterward the other virgins came also, saying, "Lord, Lord, open to us!" But he answered and said, "Assuredly, I say to you, I do not know you." Watch therefore, for you know neither the day nor the hour in which the Son of Man is coming. (Matthew 25:10-12)

Now is the time to minister to Jesus, before it's too late.

- Minister to Jesus -

1. It will require self-sacrifice to become part of the bride of Christ.

2. The bride will prepare for the wedding supper by obeying God's word.

- Prayer -

Dear God, I desire to be a part of your bride. I want to hear your voice and follow you. Help me exalt you above all. Help me to live the rest of my time on this earth in a way that is pleasing to you, so that my life is under your authority and has eternal significance. Fill me with your Spirit so that I can serve you and represent you to this broken world. I know that nothing else and no one else is worth it. I renounce everything in me that hinders me from fulfilling your glorious purpose in me. Have your way in my life. Let your bride arise, and cause me to be a part of her. In Jesus' name I pray. Amen.

Visit

www.bethelcornerstone.org

More books by Peter John Brooks:

7 Foundations

Spiritual Technology

Where God is King

The Coming Glory

Goat Tags

Absurd Christianity